WITHDRAWN
UTSA LIBRARIES

Good Trembling

Also by Baron Wormser
The White Words

Good
Trembling

Baron Wormser

Houghton Mifflin Company · Boston
1985

LIBRARY
The University of Texas

Copyright © 1985 by Baron Wormser

All rights reserved. No part of this work may be reproduced
or transmitted in any form or by any means, electronic or
mechanical, including photocopying and recording, or by any
information storage or retrieval system, except as may be expressly
permitted by the 1976 Copyright Act or in writing from the
publisher. Requests for permission should be addressed in
writing to Houghton Mifflin Company, 2 Park Street, Boston,
Massachusetts 02108.

Library of Congress Cataloging in Publication Data

Wormser, Baron.
  Good trembling.

  I. Title.
PS3573.O693G6 1985   811'.54   84-15728
ISBN 0-395-36246-6
ISBN 0-395-37725-0 (pbk.)

Printed in the United States of America

Q 10 9 8 7 6 5 4 3 2 1

Certain poems in this book first appeared in the following publica-
tions: *Agni Review:* "My Old Man," "An Art of Remoteness";
American Scholar: "Walk"; *Georgia Review:* "Werewolfness";
MSS: "The Suicide's Father"; *New England Review:* "Europe";
North American Review: "Pets"; *Paris Review:* "The Oxymoron
as Taoist Vision," "Good Trembling," "Essay: The Hudson
River School"; *Partisan Review:* "Well-Being"; *Poetry:* "Shards,"
"In baseball," "Annuals," "I Try To Explain to My Children a
Newspaper Article Which Says That According to a Computer
a Nuclear War Is Likely To Occur in the Next Twenty Years,"
"For My Brother Who Died Before I Was Born"; *Poetry East:*
"Fishing," "Letter from the Countryside," "The Fall of the
Human Empire"; *Sewanee Review:* "Poem to the Memory of
H. L. Mencken," "Getting Ready"; *Southern Review:* "The
American Intelligentsia"; *Tendril:* "By-Products"; *Virginia
Quarterly Review:* "The Delegates," "Families."

LIBRARY
The University of Texas
At San Antonio

For my father,
   Sylvan Wormser
And to the memory of my mother,
   Marcia Wormser

Word to the Reader

It is a commonplace that poems (or stories or novels or plays) stand or fall on their own merits; intention, in this world, will never be equivalent to action. This is healthy and just: there is, after all, no poetry without poems. Often, however, the judgments we make as to this or that poem distract us from the broader imperatives of poetry. A larger judgment is called for than the daisy petals of "I like it, I don't like it." For poetry offers truths which are applicable to all people and which can be incorporated into all our lives. These truths rarely are simple ones but they offer a context upon which life can lean. It is not for the poet to impose. In a nuclear age, the spectre of catastrophe casts a disquieting light upon life for any man or woman. It is hard to avoid the sense of a common human fate. What poetry offers is the courage to acknowledge a sympathy for the human predicament without which there can be no meaningful life — or, in our age, any life at all. That predicament is larger than you or me, but it is not larger than poetry. I offer these poems as pledges of what we share.

Contents

III

I

Friday Night

Dinner winds down, and the bottom
Of the accompanying bottle appears
With the abruptness of a smile
Or a plainclothesman's badge. The people
Are friends. The moments are idle as jewels.
It is not written into any constitution or
Call to arms but this takes place all over the world.
Praise to conviviality!
Praise to the flesh of the broiled fish!
Praise to the ardor that dissipates
In words and cigarettes!
These evenings are accomplishments —
That is why they disappear.
The hostess hunches over the table,
Shakes her head, speaks rapidly.
The host flips an apple into the air.
Everyone has lived through another work week,
Everyone has a story to tell:
Tanks, jokes, sickness, boots.
Myths are not dead. This is the table
Of life — one and many, human.
It is worth the journey.

Stitches

On a table in the front yard of a house
By the highway selling "odds 'n' ends"
Is something not made on any day shift —
Handkerchiefs embroidered with flowers,
Hearts, quarter moons, houses, ducks.

They are not beautiful but they are pretty
And better than anything they are someone's
Precious time — be it by a window or in
A little attic room or on a veranda — they
Are someone's time which you can see
In each little stitch that is too small to see
But is there the way the funny yellow ducks
Are there or the purplish five-petal flowers.

I pay two dollars for the lot of them,
This quiet work that did not have to be done.

Each moment in them is straight and steady and
You can see that a hand is a body
And a body is a life and a life is
The habit of time and seems, to someone who
Happens by later like this, the remainder of design.

My Children's Rooms

Nothing here can fly or walk.
Artless and uninsistent,
These toys remain where they were.
Duration is fragile —
My son likes the sound
Of plastic breaking,
My daughter buries her dolls.

On the walls there are pictures
Of dogs, mermaids, mountains,
Gymnasts, outfielders, whales.

I try to recall
What was chosen,
What was won,
What was found.

Already the children have
Such long and attributed lives!
So much has lapsed
Or abjectly been retired.
So much is done.

Before these histories
Of inclination
I feel abashed.
Like it or not
Nothing a mind touches
Is random.
Dutifully a nutcracker soldier
Regards me.
I know every little thing
But none of the large ones.

Elvis Presley

Charlene, the oldest of your sisters,
Looks into her tequila twister
And somberly relates
To you and me and the cat and the egg-smeared plates
The accidental suicide of the king.
No one could do a thing
About it because the pauper had become a prince.
No one has known what to do since.
We go upstairs to get away from her
Lugubrious lewdness, but as we murmur
And groan I can hear the music downstairs,
A thick, rising honey. You say you don't care
About me anymore. I reflect
That society is the time between sex.
There's a lurch, a clatter, and a weak shout.
I step over Charlene on the way out.
You have these Elvis dreams.
There is no time in-between.

Soap Opera

If each witless age creates an image of itself,
Ours is of a woman crying for help
Amid a crowd of well-groomed friends.
She is hysterical, tormented, saddened, upset.
In a few minutes she will be better

And stay that way until she cries again.
It was nothing that made her cry.
Ralph had told Joan that Bill might die.
She looks at us through the harsh light
That jumps off the linoleum and glass.

She is crying again and has locked the door.
She is not ugly or stupid or poor.
That's why she cries like this.
No one has told her what to do,
And she is forced to always look for clues,

To check the way adolescents dress and swear,
To listen to commentators
And remember the news.
She has opened the door.
Tom looks at her and smiles.

They kiss. It might be reconciliation
Or tenderness or thoughtless urge.
Adroit music surges over the throw rugs
And well-waxed tiles. We are convinced.
Happiness is the best of styles.

Shards

It seems sometimes as if they left all of a sudden,
A scant hour or two ahead of marauding troops
Or a hurricane — but that is only how it seems.
In fact, they were mired in their half-baked dreams.

America, after all, has never been
A country for invasions; no one has had to fight
For his home as if tomorrow it might be sacked.
Our trepidations have always been more abstract.

These people were not menaced. Their lives were
Interrupted only by a prosperity that did not
For some reason or other include them.
All these people knew — and knew it like the phlegm

In their throats or the warts on the backs of their hands —
Was that they had been robbed, although they didn't know
By whom. The fact sufficed — they'd been robbed.
And so they opened the back door and lobbed

Their busted crockery out into the night,
Letting it fall where it would. There was no point
In bothering with a broken piece of clay.
It was as expendable as the next day

Or the day after that. They were stubborn
People and poor and now there is nothing
Of their place but what they threw out. The detritus has
    remained
While the cellar hole is a sea of raspberry canes

And the elm trees are dead and the cistern has filled
Up with mice and leaves. Bits of cups, kettles, and bowls
Are everywhere, enjoying their indomitable lot,
Stolidly ignoring the good graces of rot.

The country was gone by the time these people showed up.
On the calendar it was 1926.
You can imagine them out on their tumbledown
Porch, staring at the ads for towns

In Florida and cars and stylish clothes.
The day lilies bloomed and the phoebes returned
Each spring and there was moonlight, wind, and rain
Enough. The daughters fretted, the sons complained.

One fall they had to beg the shells
To poach some deer. A banker came around.
The phoebes worried over their chicks. The country was gone;
For the people there was only the moving on.

Walk

Fond of vague, local expeditions, we
    Decide to go for a walk.
The elms are lifeless. The clouds are magenta.
        We talk
    About the prospects for disarmament,
My back pains, how in Maine each spring is "late."
        None of this
        Precipitates any debate
On the part of the woodpeckers or frost-spilled walls
    Or the hillside's seasonal waterfalls.
After a while our voices have had enough of themselves,
        We listen
    And in our aimless footsteps detect something else,
        Something lulling and May-sweet.
        We try to repeat ourselves but fail.
The gloss of description or the extraction of a moral
        Won't do.
    Notions of grandeur and humility pale.
      We sense the vacant truth:
        Peace is a motion.
We head back home through the beech grove and unfurling
    ferns.
    We are learning what we can't learn.
        On the path
        Between silence and talk
        We are learning to walk.

---

for Janet

Well-Being

A visit to the chiropractor, an extra
Glass of sherry, Boswell before bed;
Thus inspired by well-being, I stir the mundane.
Here are messages and little causes in
A language I half understand, that of
Half-neural, half-domesticated man. What was
Outside me enters, what was inside disappears.
I remain whole, an environment whose ignorance is
A government, one who is susceptible
To sneezing, falling, gulping,
Being warm or nearsighted or tall.
In the dark before sleep I recall
That the un-Johnsonian mind of latter centuries
Says nothing is there, that the body
Is an object of time put in motion by
A few imperious words and stilled
By a few obedient lies.
The gropings of appetite, all our dumb ritual rounds
Are subsumed beneath a more logical suffering —
Yet a certain dignity refuses to concede.
Bodies pose questions too.
How else, they ask, are we to consort with our
Perishing? How else to admit we are
Our own preludes? The belly roars.
The Doctor reaches across the table
And lays hands on what is good.

Poem to the Memory of H. L. Mencken

After I read you, I thought of every mortal
As a mammoth, a stewpot of provocation,
A snuffling barbarian. I liked your antidote —
Our civilization wanted dictionaries and beer.

I see you at your typewriter, bemused and irascible,
Unappalled by yesterday's perishable headlines,
Appalled by the unbridled asininity of some current
Maker of the so-called news. Journalism was the brine
Of celebrity. There were more fools than there was time.

You had a wit's distrust of higher things.
The surest proof of God you could make out
Was the existence of so many God-fearing louts.

As for the republic, it was ever-foundering —
That was what made it a republic.
The genius of democracy as you saw it
Was that it gave each simpleton, plutocrat,
Tub-thumper, hack, and two-bit hood
The chance to make as big a spectacle of himself
As he could.

You lived through Niagaras of rhetoric,
Dropped cigar ash on all the reputations of the era,
Blew smoke into America's self-satisfied eyes.

You were a Baltimoron, *adulte terrible,* and crank.
You winked. We understood.
For the great body harried daily by desire and need,
There remained the solace of good prose and good food.

There never was a bad year for crabs in Maryland.
There never was a moment when the word palled —
Until the brain blew up
And you died before your death.

Like a gap-toothed siren, the world called.
Fine, vulgar man, you got your fill.

In baseball

Neither forces nor bodies equivocate:
Each action holds a telltale trait,
Each moment convokes an actual fate.

Reality, being precious, becomes a game
In which, nature-like, no two things are the same —
Whatever is remarkable is nicknamed.

The untitled fan applauds the grace of epithet
And thinks of warring Greeks, whose threats,
Stratagems, confusions, deeds, though met

On a smaller scale, are yet quiveringly real.
Player against player on a simple field,
It's the keenness of conflict that appeals

To the citizen so sick of the abstract "they."
Here, there is no such thing as a beggared day.
Achievement can be neither created nor feigned

And the whole mix of instinct, confidence, wit,
And strength emerges as a catch or a hit,
Something indicative, legible, quick,

And yet as much a mystery as luck.
Lured by the tangible we strive to pluck
The meaning that cannot be awe-struck.

The exemplary fact remains — a ball,
The thing that rises and abjectly falls,
The unpredictable, adroit rhyme of it all.

---

for Tom Hart

Snow

I feel generous and calm in the snow.
It is a peace I understand —
Plausible, material, insistently bland.
Like imagination, it comes and goes,
An inscrutability I can be thankful for.
Like a vacationer, I am pointedly free:
I happened by, I could feel and see,
I left by a path and came through a door.

The tale is told and night will fall —
But not like this snow which has its own time.
Possible and perennial, these flakes are the lines
Of a deathbed actor, some lost speech recalled
And recited for any who still are there,
For the graying light and quivering air.

I Have the Summer Names

I have the summer names
But that seems a small reward
To one who wants the motions
That will include not only winter
And death but the eons and stars
To which words are appended
As a gaze and vestigial tail.

I will strut my dismay here
While the buzz of July endures
And caresses and chides.
I will despise all symbols
As conveyances of immobile entity,
As statues of belief.
I will watch as the tree swallow spires
Into the sky
Until it seems lost
In a space that moves timelessly.
I will rest at that invisible sight.

On perfect wings the bird returns.
I rise from the chaise lounge on which
I reclined, a casual Heraclitan who will
Take the impermanent for our permanent home
And speak not summarily
But as one who is partial, assuaged by marvel,
Gulping my breath, and going
As all creatures are going
Into winter, into the flicker
Of death.

Getting Ready

Clouds, nightfall, empty cups and empty chairs:
They all go to show that anything
Can set the engine of premonition off:
The eye capitulates; the architecture and career
Of a certain life gladly collapses;
The tepid, concerned moment
Grows, if not prophetic, then visionary.
What sturdier prospect is there than what might be?
Those flowering intimations are set free
And an immodest calm descends. It is later.
The trees have grown;
The butcher is stouter; the shingles are pearly gray,
As if time were an increment of simplicity.
The body too has its foreseeable degrees:
Plain age and palsy and intermittent sublimity.
The flesh would seem a sort
Of practical eternity were it not that common fate
Remains awake in the drumming heart —
What starts, finishes. It may come as
A casual surprise or as a further peak
On a corporate chart, or in chopped logic,
False inference, or in a gun.
All particular eventuality is there,
A kingdom-come where something must happen to someone.
The body agrees;
The mind, like a revolutionary in a cold-water flat,
Wonders what is to be done.

The American Intelligentsia

Some of the textbooks posture and darkly protest —
But in America there has never been such a thing.
At best, there were the Yankees of a hundred and more years ago
Who tried to make a heady wine out of wafer-like souls.
Bold reflection, it seemed, was not the republic's genius:
The unmatched prospect opened onto a wallpapered room;
The mettle that challenged kings took up the good works of
    industry.
As for Boston, it was too much of a locale for any platonic
    academy.
Left out in all eras the imagining mind became a fearful thing,
Made its own suffering myths, raised the lone man or woman
To a perishable god, vengefully consumed its faculties.
Strenuously or blandly, no one else much gave a damn.
The enormous, hosanna-inviting spaces sighed and dreamed.
It was the country where Optimism married Thrift,
Where all that famous criticism of life became an especially
    unwanted gift.
"I talk to the trees because they're the only ones
Who'll listen," said a series of disgruntled sages.
Each individual was vouched a commercial destiny.
Affinities became unfriendly. Despair was blamed on
    nonconformity.
No hard feelings of course. If some took it out
On themselves that was too bad. No one wished them
A life in hell or a less than honorable old age.
"Miraculously, the profession of letters does not exist here,"
A European wrote home. He was wrong. There was instead
That at once lonely and expansive American integrity.
Derision marred each loving proclamation.
The word might sew together life and death,
But it lacked geography, it would never be a nation.

Fishing

A poet grown acerbic
From the failings of beauty
Might say that this is
Need calling to need,
An economics of hope,
But it is nothing
That intelligent.
The people are in
Ludicrous, devout poses.
The fish are curious, appetitive
Because curiosity is
An appetite worse than hunger.

No person understands a fish.
A fish lacks clouds, pharmacology,
But it is interesting to be able
To be wet all the time,
Submersed in something more
Than atmosphere, purely dull,
Delightfully uncautionary.
The hook fails or it succeeds.
There are other fish,
Also unseeable, unknowable,
Yet catchable as a phrase.
We open two tepid beers
And drink to all
This easygoing, observant faith.
The line goes out over the water,
Sinks. Occasion occurs. The long
Afternoon does everything but think.

Letter from the Countryside

Quite in the middle of nowhere
I have sought to discover
The extent of my ignorance
And am doing admirably.

A light-starved hawthorn
Caught among pines puts out
A few plain flowers,
And I do not grab

As once I might have at
The analogy but let
The pointless sweetness
Of the fact flood me.

The beauty of abandonment
Is no mean thing:
Goldenrod growing through
The frame of a rusted Chevy,

Listing barns, fields
(And fields are people's lives)
Routed by poplar
Effacing whole generations.

It's forlorn, the children
Grow up only to move away —
But who cares for
Packaged consolations?

Meaning stubbornly luxuriates,
The sturdy American
Weaknesses beckon:
Seeing is believing,

Remarking is thinking.
I too am a landscape.
Knowledge is a gesture
Which all things make.

Annuals

Grays, browns, mottled blacks:
Whether withered, frost-attacked
Or simply deceased, all annuals
Go into this heap from which
Others will derive
Increase.

Death has its small uses,
And you, my wife and a gardener,
Are respectful and sensibly sad.
The commands of the seed
Contained no surprise, yet
We oohed and ahhed as if
Each bloom were somehow
Unforeseen.

Though lovingly saluted,
Beauty will not be known.
The purposing bee explains nothing.
These stringy petals and
Brittle leaves bequeath no aesthetic
Moralities.

Crumble of earth and stems —
We minister to each other.
The blossom of a memory
Succumbs to its vigor but
Will revive (you say) another
Summer, displaying the calm
Insouciance of what never went
Away.

---

for Janet

II

The Oxymoron as Taoist Vision

I do not call something "wisdom"
When I can predict the next verity.
Accommodation is wearisome.
When men rehearse the consequences
Of their passions, they call it "logic."
I do not want to act as though
I know what everyone else knows.
Because we use the same words
Does not mean we have the same eyes.
A bird flew through the village this morning.
People said it was a finch, a jay, a cardinal.
One old man swore it was a magpie.
Good for all of them!
The bird goes its way and the people have
Something to talk about.
I like surprises, minglings, distances, leaps.
Magic is inveterate.
I look at my cigarette smoke.
I like to hear what you have to say
Because it is you who are saying it.
Some child is laughing at a bowl of cereal.
If you are skillful enough,
Everything may become incongruous.
Even the "progress" everyone talks about
Will start to sing and smirk and after a while
Make certain admissions.
I clap my hands
And they sound like mountains dancing.

Stock Car Racing

It makes me nervous to think about it,
Which is why I'm here.
                        Looking subdues me
And all these other people who don't have
Anything else to do on Sunday.
                        The drivers look
Like astronauts and used to be poor.
                        The guy
Next to me won't shut up about Jesus.
This is science, my buddy says
And raises his Bud in a gesture meant
To indicate a blessing upon the world of flatheads.
There is, in this century, a technical vocabulary for
Everything.
                        This going nowhere for
The sake of going, it seems poetical, though
There are corporate stickers and logos everywhere.
Through the binoculars I observe
That Ms. Lucky Strikes has an implausible,
Goat-like smile.
                        My jaw aches, and I think of
What it is like to be calm and tense at
The same time except I am not going
Around and around at a hundred fifty miles
Per hour and am glad of it.
                        How do they
Prepare themselves for it?
                        Now the Jesus freak
Is talking about the flaming death of Junior Babcock.
For some reason the noise seems louder.
A yellow Pontiac spins
Coming out of a curve and you
Can feel everybody's fear and concern
At something untoward occurring.

                                        Just like
That the driver regains control, and no one
On the track or in the stands has
Even really paused; yet we have considered the reality
Of possibility and needled by that
Knowledge we have been reborn.

John Milton Goes Flying

The earth sped away. Villages and steeples
Grew "insignificant" — the flight instructor's
Routine remark spoken through a thin smile.
His nodding student squinted like a jeweler.
The sun dazzled, the motor muttered
Over and over again some Greek phrase.
Horizontal movement was all it was,
The sort of soaring one would expect of man
Who when faced with heaven and light
Puttered, picked up an appropriate tool,
Said something comforting but trite.

Sixteen Students Hand In Stories and Poems
in Which a Violent Death Occurs

Sterility and the romance of maniacs —
That's what my students present me.
When I say that money gets rumpled
And that vermin and roaches are prospering
And that murderers aren't interesting people
But pitiful bastards who hold
Life in contempt, these late-adolescents
Exchange sage glances with one another
And expertly sigh. I tell them about
That mama's boy Rimbaud and wonder
Why life must be an extremity
To these kindly, overfed children who
Have never seen a knife wound or unembalmed corpse.
Some gravity of the psyche much stronger
Than my middling advice entices them.
I read about death-in-life and death plain.
Assassins talk philosophy. Windshields shatter.
Junior executives are strangled by ennui.
The blood on the floor isn't blood
But an avoidance of disillusion.
We must know the worst, my students say.
I give them letter grades and complain
About how no one respects the semi-colon anymore.
The idealist killer hollers an epithet, lunges.
A scream is written down.
Mediocrity gets its just rewards.

By-Products

The legion hall in Atherton contains
Three unclean couches, more than fifty uncomfortable chairs,
    Seven brands of less-than-good whiskey,
A tomcat with one glaucous eye named "Ike,"
Stagnant windowless air, and more often than not

    My legless friend, Stan, who, unlike most
Of the human race in this county and beyond, is content to go
    Unsaved. He drinks ginger ale, talks about sex
In a voice of awe and disgust, and plays cribbage
For a buck a game. "Here sits," he says sometimes

    Out of the blue and to no one special, "one of
The by-products of Vietnamization," but no one hushes up
      the way
    They used to because everyone there's a veteran
Of one sort or another, and who, in fact, knows shit
About Korea anymore or, for that matter, Tarawa

    As witnessed by Charley Levesque who, though
Here, never came home? Friday nights it's cards and some
    Mediocre eight-ball and later talk which doesn't
Always wind up back in Nam but more often hovers
Between there and here, say in some Pentagon general's

    So-called mind or a television show or a girl's
Smile at a football game fifteen years ago. Neither of us ever had
    Much talent for optimism or, for that matter,
Rage. Our insignificance lulls us, and we know it
Could all happen again, whatever it was, an obligation

Split by a moment; or as with me, a lifetime of
Moments, each one praying nothing will happen. Living is the
     job no
One's particularly good at, and some days Stan says
He feels more here than anyone, because he gave something
Up, because there's a difference between being hurt and being
     afraid.

An Art of Remoteness

From his unpardoned perch, a kitchen table
In a sunless walkup in a city
Of tangled boulevards, he tested
The old, unwieldy nemesis — namelessness.
Forgetting (he knew) couldn't be remedied
But these gestures of identity (he liked to think)
Rankled the equanimities of time:
A conceit, of course, but preferable to
The quarrels of the ego, the canter of
Description, or discoveries of the avant-garde.
To be contemporary was to be credulous —
A blessed state but a boring one too.
As a sort of Pliny the Incipient
He felt freer. The unalloyed past
Was his, and he could be — as the inclination
Importuned — a border guard,
Weak-kneed theosophist, or pure *Montagnard*.
To sketch a grammar of affinity
Was something the more well-read censors
Had sensed but about which they felt
Oddly powerless. An art of remoteness,
Un-here, un-now, provoked only shrugs.
Were Epictetus and Iphigenia to be allowed?
Did Geronimo challenge the present regime?
Was the human condition an augmented chord?
An "Ode to Notaries" won a minor award.
He went on tour to buried towns.
The random Everyman contributed footfalls
On a gravel path, boasts, the remnants of strife.
He made another cup of weak tea
And sympathized with oblivion's plight.
Across millennia life will allude to life.

My Old Man

The Fifth Plenary Congress:
That's him over in the right-hand corner,
Some grease spots on his serge lapels —
But what of it?
He'd picked up the lingo —
Cowboy dialectics, shark-tooth logic —
As well as the next boy-who-made-good.
I recall the delicacies he brought home
From the metropolis, the stolid jokes,
The newspapers that didn't misspell our name.
He got to have his teeth fixed.
He got to vacation for two weeks
At a lake stocked with trout.
He got to sign a treaty.
Falsehoods and soft beds
And at the bottom of the glass
The dregs of belief. Phooey on
The opiate of discourse. I used his
Electric razor sans rotary blade
At the age of eight. Once I took it to school.
"Look at this," I said.
"It's the revolution."

Grown

Tonight sons and daughters return
To that memory parents call "home,"
The past of place. These children, however,
Are grown; their wishes are calmly clever,
Their exclamations hyperbolically wry.
They have learned how not to cry.

Everyone talks at once; then everyone
Is still. A wary satisfaction
Takes hold. Love deepens its disguise;
Intention is veiled in surmise.
The summaries are, at once, tender and bluff.
One small sarcasm is more than enough.

To be disappointed is childish.
The old people still eat off those dishes
Dad won on the midway in forty-eight.
The young people still do not sit up straight,
Still act as though they raised themselves.
Everyone could use some unwanted help.

As for what changes, it can't be put on view
Or peremptorily told what to do.
Imperfect, it is perfect, and there seems
Something just about this talky dream
That so hopelessly stops and starts,
As if in discrepancy there were art.

The kitchen clock remains in its spot.
All can see. An awful lot
Of time has gone by. All say so.
Tedium has a comfort of its own,
And in the morning, phone calls superintend:
We must try to see each other again.

The Grain: A Conversation

Whatever he did with wood he did well —
Finessing the knots, matching the joints,
Nailing for strength. It's an art, we
Both agree, but there we halt. He says
That hands can't be passed on and that
The skill ends there with the body's fall.
His ruefulness surprises me. Tradition,
I insist, cannot stop and start.
It can't be periodically retrieved. It must
Steadily breathe. He snorts at my metaphor
And thinks of his sons — one teaches, the other
Sells machines. I was self-taught, he says.
I saved for a pocket knife, then a saw.
It never stopped. I knew the wood,
What I could do with it. Then he stops.
Why should they (thinking back to his sons)
Do what I do? He looks at me now,
Not the tools or boards. No reason, I say,
But what if this didn't die
With you? What if you were built upon?
What if what we came to know by patience
And care and a sort of love didn't
Always disappear? What if identity
Didn't tempt us to act alone?
All questions, however plainly put,
That can't be answered. All questions, he said,
That run, in this world, against the grain.

Good Trembling

"Good trembling," CJ said as we
Walked along the docksides in our thin jackets
Even though it was winter on the East Coast.
We were advertising our urge for life
To ourselves and anyone else who might
Have noticed. It wasn't likely, but we liked
To believe that our minds had lights,
That we were intellectual Tom Swifts
And pureblooded peasants of the finer and
Tumultuous emotions. A little era babbled through us.
"I don't want to become an anecdote,"
I said as I waved my arms at the thought
Of eternity — say being thirty and married.
A cop car slowed down beside us. Long hair.
"I can't imagine that," CJ said.
"It's too cold and windy." We looked straight ahead,
But the car drove off anyway.
It was warm in there for them. We got some coffee,
Exchanged barrages of quotations,
Vowed to rectify the inertia of everyone else,
And went out again into that clenched wind
Of portents, dogmas, and seasonable love.

For a Generation of Poets

Made to assume the genius of amiability,
They freighted the private moment, lived — it seemed —
For the untutored flashes of native perspicacity.

It was the freedom born of suicide and picnics,
When sensibility grew eyeless, rapt, and all-
Encompassing. Beside Géricault's smouldering *jeune homme*
Was pasted a Kodak of a short-sleeved graduate student,
Bereft of gestures,
Smiling a slight, portentous smile, as if to say,
"Here is Lycidas, drowned but alive."

Highways and millions of dollars and skies full of planes
Invented that armory of modest, brisk styles.

The facades demanded divination, the tabloids shrieked
"React, react," and in the middle of the century
Of calibrated celebration, of machine-made reverie,
Who could begrudge these heirs their disabused modernity?

No one knew better than they, the hurtful truth —
Poems are gestures swallowed by history.

We repeat their stubborn incantation:
Let us earn our ends,
Let us pretend and not pretend.

The Suicide's Father

Everything has become a museum.
Where I live is where I lived.
My face in the mirror in the morning
Was my face. I am here the way a chair
Or painting is here. I have weight and
A meaning I cannot possess.

We walked to the war plaza, bought bags
Of popcorn, watched the jugglers and mimes,
Walked home through the lamp-lit twilight.
It was a Sunday in early spring.

What do you do when the past is
No longer yours? I was a simple man.
I thought it was something that could not
Be taken away. I would have it
For always. But I have lost it.

Now in those looks, excursions, mornings —
Even in laughter — I see death.
It is wrong but that is what I see.

I have put my purposes in a bag
And thrown them into a river and watched
Them sink. It did not take long.
It is cold in that river and now when I walk
I wander like a tramp or a bored pensioner.
People avoid me or babble courteously.

You, my boy, are never mentioned.
Of course, that is for the best. I have
Committed a crime, but I am not sure
What it was. It is a crime where there
Are no police or reports or even lies.

It is a crime of meals, gifts,
Postcards, worries, lullabies.

There was the time you asked for money.
The time I didn't hear from you for months.
But we all have those times and we live
And however battered we come around.

You did not like illusions. I do not think
You liked those grimacing mimes.
I, as a father, did. I did
What a father does. I talked about you.
My son was this, my son was that.
My son built little wooden planes
That really flew. I was proud. Like the mime
Who could not open the imaginary door, you frowned.

You were in the river for a week
Before they found what they said was you.
I had to say it too.
On what was a hand was a ring.

What was there before this to ever
Think twice about? Everything. Everything.

Rockefeller

"He's a man the same as you
Or me." I was not
A man but a boy and
I knew as much to know
That it wasn't true, this "sameness"
I heard of from mechanics where
My father took his car
And bricklayers who worked
On our house and druggists who
Poured liquids all day from
One bottle into another.
Being a man then must be nothing,
I thought. It was something
You couldn't avoid and by judging it
You tried to get the better of it,
As if there were a choice involved.
Each man could be the lord
Of his mortal attitudes.
I saw grease, mortar,
Colored syrups. "You aren't him,"
I wanted to say like a clever kid
In the comics, but what would
That have done? Their dignity was
A statue on a too-small pedestal.
They said they wouldn't take off
Their hats for money and fame, but
They did. They were the same.

The Delegates

In the afternoon another apologia for savagery.
I want to doze or spit but instead am obliged
To nod courteously, disapprovingly, bemusedly —
Call it what you will for no one cares.
Everything is finite except for self-preservation.
The greed for being is the god in us.
What they call "countries" are a few lost men
And a lot of people.
The people go from day to day
Like cattle or hens. They roll their eyes and joke.
It is not demeaning, only stubborn.
The leaders sit and plot —
How to outwit death, how to build a swimming pool,
How to make up a word that is frightening and
Obsequious at the same time. They fail, but no one
Much notices because the next ones do the exact
Same thing only they paint a moustache on history or
They cross the moustache out. For us delegates
Wisdom consists of shrugs, easy sex,
And a steady what-can-you-expect whine
To greet each accusation and punctilious brag.
Sometimes out on the street one of us sees a child
Skipping rope or a young man whistling.
It is strange, and when someone
Answers, you want to believe the words.
If no one knows anything,
Then innocence is no crime.

Tutorial on the Metaphysics of Foreign Policy

The disparate days are extricably bound:
A middle-aged man writes down
The future according to the terrain of expediency,
Lights a cigarette, blows smoke nonchalantly.
— Recognize his face, the baffled frown.

The passion of circumstance
Has been linked by formalists to dance,
The drama, a game of chess that bleeds.
All true as metaphors go but dissolute —
Each country prizes its own hurt,
Grieves and postures each time for the first time.
— Recognize the ease of principled crime.

Each hero is absolute,
And the agitprop of humble needs
Proclaims the candor of salt and bread
But ignores the life of the dead,
The gravity of accustomed fate,
All the fancy of plain fear and hate
That gives imagination power.
— Recognize the blind hour.

Such feelings can't be checked
But may take the direc-
Tion an enemy or ally seeks:
The trick here is congruence,
That attitude which speaks
Of a plausible hope —
Time may accomplish what speeches invoke.
— Recognize the toast, the public joke.

As for the idol of humanity
It remains a *philosophe*'s notion,
Treacherous as the oceans
That separate these sovereign states.
— Recognize idealism's quick corruption.

The best policy upholds the traits
That ever-transform the lyric One
Into the motley Other:
A nation is never a brother,
And what comity there is, lies
Not in the occasions of surprised
Improvisation but in the labors of fact,
Those details of accord which attract
Trust and return to a ballad's refrain,
The sky on a morning of rain.
— Recognize the innocence of pain.

Without a Telescope

Tonight I bequeath to my planet an era of
Gentle forebodings, the illusion of perspicuous thought,
All the latitudes of doting, long-winded love.
It is the stars that do it, that make me on an August night
Both wishful and free. I am too far north, there is no wind,
I must see stars and know I cannot speak of what I see.
A laggard taxonomist, I notice some aspects of enormity
While others flee from me — unseeking and unsought.
Millions of years have conspired to leave me untaught.
Eyes shut, I recline and salute the inopportune mind
That makes it so easy to hold nothing so tightly,
That prinks its puny knowingness. I cannot speak clearly.
I am distant and partial and am touched nearly
By what endures in this spectacle of heedlessness.
I must be earthly. I must be the sidereal guess.

Essay: The Hudson River School

You see it especially in the paintings of
The mid-nineteenth century — that serene, beckoning distance
As if they could not look too closely at what was near
Preferring instead that vista of promise
For which they became famous.
It wasn't, to be sure, those clichéd, too-contented
Objects of pastoral nor those
Mechanical obeisances to Poussin and Claude
That made the reviewers boast and declaim.
It was as the acolytes of natural sentiment
And limners of a momentous terrain that these painters
Were plausibly American.
                                        Still there are,
Even amid patriotism, certain qualities
One must take into account. Although, for instance,
The figures in their pictures are often dwarf-small,
They do not seem humbled. They labor intently,
Or they gaze and take the measure of that misty
Enormity spread out before them. The mind has a scale
Of its own, and this must be a country of enterprising
Citizens. Politics, for once, will have eyes.
In the middle ground there are a series of perfect planes
Whose grandeur is orderly:
The mountains sit like deacons;
A lake lies limp as a cloth.
Each tree is the image of a tree.
We behold the forest of an actual, Edenic patrimony.
We cannot live there and wouldn't want to
But cherish it as a moral charm.
Then there is that distance which although aerial
Avoids heaven. Sensation is uncertain,
But what's far away comforts and murmurs
And gently speculates. Remoteness means no harm,
And these are the landscapes of a thorough mercy,
A sublime but imaginable grace.

In the Suburbs: An Adolescence

Perhaps the absence of destiny was destiny.
Amid the barbered lawns, roadways, Valhallas
Of brick-facing and glass,
The mind stretched, vaulted, and gnawed.
Each silly thought became a victory,
Each eager wage earner a personality.
The play of the breeze on the cement-lined "pond"
Seemed an unregenerate eccentricity.
The geranium stuck in a too-big clay pot
Was emblematic, eternal, and dire red.
Car-like, words went somewhere
And it was up to me to stop the soporific
Economy of half-intercourse,
To sing loudly and badly, to invent nicknames,
To play the unredeemed fool.
I convinced myself of my necessity
And was ignored by all.
How perfect each thing was!
Even in dreams I failed to rob my neighbors
Of their material dignity.
Awake, I had no achieved desires
But sat in a cheerful room and read another book
About the depths of human effrontery.

The Mowing Crew

The mourners drive away
And talk about the graves.

Old man Shorey can't
Keep the mowing boys at work.
They take off
Their shirts and lie in the sun
Beside their machines
And go to sleep.

Young as they
Are, the grass doesn't bother them.
Their hair is girl-long,
They smile and spit.

Even when one of their own
Dies with his car on
The state highway, they don't
Seem to exactly believe it.

Standing at the graveside
They look placidly
At the dark, riven ground
And nod to each other
As if it were another
Hot day and they felt
Drowsy and wished to lie down.

A Deciduous Poem

The other day I had a longing for some boiled irony.
It is a not uncommon craving and one which, according to
The literature of self-help, may be indulged deliberately.
How fine it is not to wear a hair shirt, nor have one's
Knuckles smashed by a hammer, nor discuss the fascist
Undercurrents of bourgeois ideology.
Instead I can sit in a café and exhale mentholated smoke.
There is no crevice too small for a person to fit.
I have read of a people who make their homes
From fallen leaves.
Most of the day they dance or sleep.
If I wait long enough there will be another new order.
Then I may be on the right side and have a desk
And a farmgirl turned secretary.
People always think if you are cheerful you are masquerading
Some anguish.
I want to think about the soccer scores.
I want to eat the flavors and ignore the gross foods.
I want to sing saxophone.
Soon it will be dusk which, if you have noticed, is a signal.
In the streets you will see men and women trudging home
Alongside gutters heaped with fallen leaves.

III

A Diary from the Territories

Each hearth was a thought of dominion;
Each riven log an idyll's death.
The raccoon gawked, the deer fled
Before the assertion of a destined estate.

Each neighbor watched his neighbor's fate.
Each mirror possessed a familiar face.
Timber-like each sentence was hewn.
Each mind was the same, purposeful place.

The habit of fortitude impaled more
Than one unacknowledged heart;
Despite the fierce work, life did
Little more than perennially start.

In cold spring the daffodils rose one by one.
A spider in summer devoured,
As the children watched, a crippled fly.
In the sky a hollow moon

Distributed a thin and incxact light.
The day over, smoke dwindled above
The chimney, an old cat fitfully slept,
A pen went searching through the night.

Europe

Again and again in the twilit parlor
Memory measured once-passionate affinities.
Amid the oils of swains and kings, *objets d'art*,
And numerous appurtenances never before seen
In a western Massachusetts hill town,
One tried to grasp the pure, reducible thing,
The inclination which had no local correlative.
The voyagers intoned their heuristic thoughts —
Comparisons and questions more often than not:
What did one think of Bernini, Van Eyck, the Ring?
What was there about a Roman spring?
The snow dripped from the eaves in lackadaisical drops
While the guest, a pilgrim of sorts, made
At intervals, avowals as to the world-at-large.
Wise looks were proferred with the cream and tea.
Who, after all, wanted to live and die
Without having tasted sublimity?
What was the point of all this endless, obscure
Making? When would America be done?
Each day went by undefined in a town about
Which, because it was American, one could
Say only that it was like any other town.
One wanted repose, brilliance, beauty, grace.
Instead one made these visits and listened as
Each chosen word decried the poverty of
Mere time and place: eternity was worldly,
Tradition owned a profounder eye. Gaffer Reilly asked
One day at the stable what did it matter what
Such people thought? Wasn't the Pope a dago?
From their hill they could see the *campagna*
As if it were yesterday. The heat
Of the New England summer seared
The very dust. In the doorway beside Goethe's bust
Civilization said goodbye. Later, on the way
Down Elm Street, other meanings seemed meant.
The deep, autumnal night intimated a continent.

The Fall of the Human Empire

When a dog is struck by a car,
A civilization collapses. A bystander
Explains this lack of allegory
As the dog whines about its accidental pain,
Wobbles, and lurches. It is a gray afternoon
In the city. This shorthaired mongrel
Is not a bomb or a lie.
Two cars stop, and a student on the way home
From the public library thinks of how
Chekhov could see the world through the eyes
Of a dog. "No one believes me" —
That is the miserable thought which is
The sonata of these confusions. Clarity
Is equivalent to pain in this world.
Even a writhing dog, who is not Chekhov,
Could tell you that. There needs to be
An official for this compromising situation.
There needs to be an economy.
Dogs are like habits. This one sobs
And tries to drag itself somewhere else.
In operas people sing with all their hearts
About a missing loveletter or a shoe.
The world cannot be quiet any longer
About this dog. The peril is too great.
Silence is a dictator who lets you live
Today so you can be killed tomorrow.
Don't fool yourself.
This dog is unimportant as you.

I Try To Explain to My Children
A Newspaper Article Which Says
That According to a Computer
A Nuclear War Is Likely To Occur
in the Next Twenty Years

Death (I say) used to have
Two faces: one good, one bad.
The good death didn't like to do it —
Kill people, dogs, insects, flowers —
But had to do it. It was his duty.
He would rather have been playing cards.
Without him the earth would get too crowded,
The soil would become tired, feuds would
Overtake love. That was what death
Believed — and when we thought about it
We agreed.
        The bad death was a bully.
He would kill angels if he could.
He settled for children, poets,
All flesh increased by spirit.
He bragged and made bets and said
Disparaging things about the human race.
People made his job easy, he said.
They were full of a confusion that
Soon became hatred. He would shake
His head in wonder, but he understood.
The nations of the world offered him
Their love.
        The new death doesn't
Have a face. He will kill us but
In the meantime he wants to kill life too.

He is calm, devoted, gradual.
He is crazy. The other two deaths
Do not like him, the way he wears
A tie as if death were an office,
The way he wants to be efficient.
Fate and fortune bore him. He has
Reasons. There cannot be enough death,
He says. You will put us out of business,
The other two say, but he doesn't listen.
Things seem the same, my children, but
They aren't.

Press Conference

Blame is better than thought,
A smile is better than a sigh,
The past is safer than the present.
A squad of pencils underlines "hard-fought."

Rituals exist which no wit
May demystify or profane.
Carefully nothing will be said;
A cordial distance will explain

Itself with choice imprecision.
Elsewhere a cat jumps off a chair,
A light flashes, a thin voice screams.
The modulations of predecision

Gut all nagging fears.
This is the preferable dream,
And would sit like a sipping king
And wisely neither see nor know nor hear.

"The Essay"

Handicapped, according to the professors,
By the absence of theory,
He shyly labored for years over a few pages
Of halting prose in which, bare-bones,
He meant to define his shifting art.
He'd invented what already existed —
But that was hard to plainly set out.
After a sentence or so, some metaphor set in.
He winced and tried again.
"The essay" became a family joke,
A regimen, an attitude.
At times, it made him playfully dark.
If everything is something else,
There is no clarity or certainty
Or duration or truth.
Confusion then is commonsense
And this shrewd sorting, this foray
Of likelihood, this cautious letting go
Was all a way of saying, "I know that
I don't know."
In the meantime there were poems
And the not unwanted awareness
That it did him good to open occasionally
His top drawer and take out that
Tangled text and stare for an hour
Past the *as-if* of things
To that more unimaginable place,
That death-in-life of definite words.

ICCO: Intellectual Construction Company

I wanted to change the world
But couldn't stand the smell in the streets.
Instead I had perspicuous thoughts.
I spoke only when spoken to,
Mouthed the same banalities over and over again.
In these insincerities I felt like a criminal.
When would they realize that I
Was not one of them, that I was unconvinced?
I had no image of my rise and did not fear my fall.
I lacked a motto and studied disenchantment.
Salesmen would come into the office to
Sell the company some concrete.
"What good is your concrete?" I wished to say.
"Who cares if there are more bridges,
Highways, jetports? What is the point of going places
When you aren't happy no matter where you are?
Why are you destroying the earth?"
The salesmen sucked on mouth-freshening mints
And squeezed my limp hand. I read Nietzsche
At lunch over my hamburger and Coke.
The mark of teleology was on me. I didn't
Even shrug. Employees called me up with stories.
One's wife had run away, one's wife had come back,
One had lost his car, one had bought a car.
Whatever it was, they needed money.
I said I would tell the boss
When he got back from Milwaukee. I posted
Bail money three times and wondered how people
Got into such troubles. The secretaries downstairs
Kept smiling at me. What was I doing carrying that book
With me? Did I mean to hit someone with it?
They talked for hours about their friends' friends.

The world was too interesting. I stared at a calendar
That advertised prestressed reinforced cement piers.
Outside, maple blossoms fell and became crushed against
The sidewalk and began to decay in the rain.
I wondered if it was possible to escape my unbuilding mind.

On a Postcard of a Matisse Painting
Taped to a Refrigerator Door

At your age this display indicates
Neither theoretical statement nor wry, sensual intent
But something more modest and proficient — love.
The card waggles in the breeze,
Lifts when the door swings.
The better to see you, the porcelain white
All around proclaims —
And it is true, there is no avoiding
This presence of red and blue.
It is a painting of some of a room,
A mockery of walls.
I propose
That location is an act of taste,
And size an artifice imposed
On acquiescent space.
My words make a museum.
You laugh. Any beauty is adequate,
You say.
You've got to work in the morning;
We sit at your table
And glimpse this card,
This small but timeless holiday.

Song: I Thought I Must Notice

Time ran out the back door.
I thought to stop it and said,
"You are my daughter and son.
You cannot end what only's
    Just begun."

In the garden, footprints;
The comical leaps of toads.
I heard the faithful phoebe sing
And I thought I must notice
    That it was spring.

On the bureau, instamatic
Evocations of our stalwart dust.
In a sleepless bed, castles of thoughts,
Outings, names. How could it be
    I too was caught?

Endings were an arrogance
I was happy to surrender.
All afternoon my children intently play.
Behind sadness I glimpse the trickster,
    Forthright day.

Words to a Mourner

At the bottom of the stair,
   Is a stair
That has no bottom.

   You must walk there.

At the height of a day
   Is an hour
That disappears.

   You must stay there.

Beyond what-might-have-been
   Is a hope
That blossoms like breath.

   You must test it.

After the tottering and fall
   Is a knowledge
That spares no little life.

   You must respect it.

---

for D. L. and S. L.

The Language Gains

It was democracy, that palpable abstraction,
(De Tocqueville later recollected in quietude)
Which, conductor-like, produced
Such a farrago of declarations, brags,
Tonic speechifyings, rapt insinuations —
All to no apparent purpose. For the hell of it.
Within that treadmill of assertion only
Sheer tone transfigured all those repeatable names.
The ever-wrangling parties were agreed:
No two parvenus were the same.

More authoritative manners might silently
Stare, but without the vaunt of the personal
What ever could be discovered? Inspiration
Would languish. There would be no accidents —
Happy or unhappy — no locales.
History would fall like windless snow.

If even now these articulations seem excessive,
As when some pure product announces in
A deformed, naturalist lingo that he
Or she has an intuition never before revealed,
Then remember that the language gains
Something with each stumbling re-annunciation.
There is a discourse beyond dialectics.
Time would be available. Definition can't be saved.
Freedom is so much eloquent noise.

Pets

As lives sprout purposes, animals will enter
And persist. Glimpsed, saluted, fed and stroked,
Like philosophers' notions they persevere
Serenely when we are off elsewhere.
Their needs are what we make them out to be.
They take affection when it is proferred
And stand up well to the occasional scrutiny
They are subject to — that "How is it then with you?"
Which we like to ask at some impertinent,
Wobbly moment, our vacancy focused
On the plight of the unwitting. They scratch an itch,
Roll over, wag a tail, belch, and we return
To our ways, for once not tempted to be importunate.
Their deaths are crises. Such a placidity
Of being, flowing parallel to all our starts
And stops and stutters is comforting. They seemed
To have found out a secret that they were not choosing
As yet to reveal. They were there, and there, and when
They are gone it becomes clear, that something
Homemade and approachable has disappeared.

Sunday Review Section

Beneath the marmalade, muffins, and tea
Sits this placemat of tendentious summary —
Apollinaire, Babe Ruth, why the Kaiser fought:
Someone is thinking what should be thought
And saying it in just so many paragraphs.
The flag of self-expression is at half-mast —
Cannily reverential, limp, but self-aware.
Like the toaster, history stands in need of repair.

After a while, you get to know each sort
Of fixer — the genteel sage who holds the fort
While the mob makes ever more awful demands;
The convert who publicly washes his or her hands
Of human error; the Cato of the commonweal;
The mortgaged drone; the cultured actress; the real
Latest academic hotshot; the slob; the memoirist
Who shouldn't tell but can't resist.

The table becomes sticky with received perceptions,
Hedged complaints, and wrong-headed questions.
Sated, the eye considers a sky perplexed
With clouds, a brimming landscape unvexed
By the mysteries of interpretation.
The mind feels something like elation.
A little butter remains on a crust of bread;
The living succeed, and the dead remain dead.

Concerning a Victim of
the Mid-Century Persecutions

In the early mornings
He drafted petitions concerning his "unmemorable demise"
To the local Chamber of Commerce; Frances Perkins;
The Demiurge of Americanism, Mickey Mantle —
But mailed none.
Beyond all the wrong turns of his life,
There was a further twist:
Mail couldn't be sent by someone who didn't exist.
He breakfasted on these casual impossibilities.
It wasn't, after all, his mind or sense
Of humor he'd lost but only his arcane vocation — physicist.
Freed from the gravity of theory,
He'd risen into a world without doubts.
The right to experiment, it turned out,
Was a political gift, and one for which,
As the newspapers put it, he was "particularly unfit."
"Dear J. Edgar Hoover,
This is to announce that I am no longer a man
But have become something more real —
I am a fear."
By means of photographs, fingerprints, and a few
Prosaic lies, he'd publicly been hypostatized.
His affinities became facts.
He was faithless.
Like his data, he deserved to disappear.
He'd driven cabs, worked the night shift,
And once for seven months tarred asphalt roofs
With two Sicilians who never spoke but to swear.
He'd learned about whatever
He'd never known. His senses remained his own,
And he could tell the weather from the movements of birds,
Sleep out-of-doors, befriend stray dogs.
He knew which churches had soup and beds

And which fed you the kingdom-to-come.
Suffering was the most spurious form of wisdom.
The world through which he ghosted went from one hell
To another. Those secrets he might have divined were gone.
"Who pulls your strings, you Red bastard?"
Knowledge exists in relation to everything,
And life is a sentiment that's easily set
On fire. Sometimes at night in his rented room
He thought of the precision of energy. Matter hissed
With purpose. He dreamt of sleep.

Werewolfness

The sizable literature more or less agrees:
The beast loves the first scream best,
The one when its face first becomes plain.
Fluorescence will do, but moonlight is best.

There is to the distressed something horribly
Natural about such an inordinate event.
At nighttime anything can occur.
Fear grows familiar; imagination relents.

Is the victim a victim?
Will the moment remain vividly impaled?
Could astonishment rebound
And grab the half-thing by its unlikely tail?

After possibility comes identity —
A letdown, but nothing stays forever new.
Its brief glory past, the creature
Does indifferently what it never wanted to do.

Families

Father John picked the baby up and whirled
About with her, lost her, picked her up
Tenderly and began dancing again, a sort
Of lumbering waltz, lost her, lost her. . . .
To look into his eyes was to see gentleness
On fire, despondent love. We turned away
But the night windows showed us our own domestic
Wilderness. Recitals, impatience, weary facts,
Awakenings in the craw of the marauding night —
No one exactly screamed. Life isn't like that.
It was more a matter of those looks. You could
See the secret coming. You knew there'd be hell to pay,
But hell never gets definitively paid.
Flesh and blood soothes; Mama Kate could
Sing a song to make you weep, about nothing really —
A meadow mouse, a cloud, a doll made of straw.
All that fitful mercy infected us.
It could make you believe in God or your wedding day
Or even being big yourself, having children
And kissing them and frowning because the two never
Get untangled, the hand that teases you will beat
You too. Some days we go down to the river and
We lie on the rocks and enjoy the simpleness of it,
Just bodies, not a sister or brother. Old strap welts
Pale in the sun and when other people talk
To you it doesn't seem so bad that they'll
Never know. Because you wouldn't want them to.
What's familiar is special. What's intimate is
Something undecided — half-kindly, half-cruel.

For My Brother Who Died
Before I Was Born

Pearly and opaque boy, it was you
To whom as a god
I furtively prayed before
I launched an aggie
Or played a decisive card.

I made lists of the reasons why:
Certain teachers and times of the year
And the failure of my team
To score runners from third —
Those were all things to make you die.

I meant to discover
My own mortality.
I mocked my mocking breath
And deftly smoked
Too many cigarettes.
At night I heard footsteps, high-pitched
Voices. Once I saw a face in a candle flame.

Your absence was a game
Which might at any move
Intrude upon my wanting life.
My hand fit in your old ball glove.
My dream was real:
Imagination is the proof of love.